Dear Parents and Educators,

Welcome to Penguin Young Readers! As parents and educators, you know that each child develops at his or her own pace—in terms of speech, critical thinking, and, of course, reading. Penguin Young Readers recognizes this fact. As a result, each Penguin Young Readers book is assigned a traditional easy-to-read level (1–4) as well as a Guided Reading Level (A–P). Both of these systems will help you choose the right book for your child. Please refer to the back of each book for specific leveling information. Penguin Young Readers features esteemed authors and illustrators, stories about favorite characters, fascinating nonfiction, and more!

Pocahontas: An American Princess

LEVEL **4**

GUIDED READING LEVEL **O**

This book is perfect for a **Fluent Reader** who:
• can read the text quickly with minimal effort;
• has good comprehension skills;
• can self-correct (can recognize when something doesn't sound right); and
• can read aloud smoothly and with expression.

Here are some **activities** you can do during and after reading this book:
• Comprehension: After reading this book, answer the following questions.
    • What did Pocahontas's name mean in the language of her people?
    • What did the native people receive from the Englishmen for trading baskets of corn and oysters?
    • Why did the native people take John Smith as a prisoner?
    • Why did Powhatan refuse the crown that the English king had sent?
    • How did Pocahontas's actions save John Smith two separate times?
    • Why did John Smith wait so long to visit Pocahontas in England?
• Character's Feelings: In this story, Pocahontas experiences excitement and disappointment. Reread the story and identify the parts where Pocahontas experiences these feelings. Pretend you are Pocahontas. Would you feel the same way as her? Why or why not?

Remember, sharing the love of reading with a child is the best gift you can give!

—Bonnie Bader, EdM
  Penguin Young Readers program

*Penguin Young Readers are leveled by independent reviewers applying the standards developed by Irene Fountas and Gay Su Pinnell in *Matching Books to Readers: Using Leveled Books in Guided Reading*, Heinemann, 1999.

For Jackie H—SH

Penguin Young Readers
Published by the Penguin Group
Penguin Group (USA) Inc., 375 Hudson Street, New York, New York 10014, USA
Penguin Group (Canada), 90 Eglinton Avenue East, Suite 700, Toronto, Ontario M4P 2Y3, Canada
(a division of Pearson Penguin Canada Inc.)
Penguin Books Ltd, 80 Strand, London WC2R 0RL, England
Penguin Ireland, 25 St Stephen's Green, Dublin 2, Ireland (a division of Penguin Books Ltd)
Penguin Group (Australia), 707 Collins Street, Melbourne, Victoria 3008, Australia
(a division of Pearson Australia Group Pty Ltd)
Penguin Books India Pvt Ltd, 11 Community Centre, Panchsheel Park, New Delhi—110 017, India
Penguin Group (NZ), 67 Apollo Drive, Rosedale, Auckland 0632, New Zealand
(a division of Pearson New Zealand Ltd)
Penguin Books (South Africa), Rosebank Office Park, 181 Jan Smuts Avenue,
Parktown North 2193, South Africa
Penguin China, B7 Jiaming Center, 27 East Third Ring Road North,
Chaoyang District, Beijing 100020, China

Penguin Books Ltd, Registered Offices: 80 Strand, London WC2R 0RL, England

Text copyright © 2000 by Joyce Milton. Illustrations copyright © 2000 by Shelly Hehenberger.
All rights reserved. First published in 2000 by Grosset & Dunlap, an imprint of Penguin Group (USA) Inc.
Published in 2013 by Penguin Young Readers, an imprint of Penguin Group (USA) Inc.,
345 Hudson Street, New York, New York 10014. Manufactured in China.

Library of Congress Control Number: 00061733

ISBN 978-0-448-42181-0   10 9 8 7 6 5 4 3 2 1

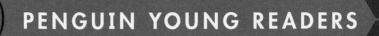

POCAHONTAS
AN AMERICAN PRINCESS

by Joyce Milton
illustrated by Shelly Hehenberger

Penguin Young Readers
An Imprint of Penguin Group (USA) Inc.

Pocahontas lived in the wild forests of Virginia. She loved to swim in the clear streams.

She could swing on the thick grapevines
that hung from the tallest trees.
In the language of her people,
her name meant playful, or fun-loving.

5

Sometimes Pocahontas helped the older women weave baskets. She learned to decorate clothes with beads and porcupine quills. But Pocahontas didn't have to work very hard. Her father, Powhatan, was a great chief.

Chief Powhatan lived in a village called Weromocomoco (say: Wee-row-mow-co-ma-co). He had a dozen wives. He had 30 children. But Princess Pocahontas was his favorite.

One day a messenger arrived with big news. Three huge ships had come from across the sea. The ships were so big that the native people called them "floating islands."

There were over 100 passengers on the ships. All of them were men and boys. They carried long sticks that shot out fire. They wore thick armor that protected them from arrows.

Chief Powhatan was curious. Who were these strangers? And what were they doing in his kingdom?

The strangers had come from England. They had set sail in the winter of 1606. It took almost five months to cross the ocean.

A few were young men who had been in trouble at home. Their families were happy to be rid of them. Others were hoping to get rich quickly. They thought they would find gold in this unknown land.

At first, all went well. The Englishmen built a walled fort called Jamestown. The native people were called Indians by the settlers. They were happy to trade baskets of corn and oysters for pretty glass beads, needles, and metal pins.

But soon, there was trouble. The strangers and the native people didn't speak the same language or understand one another's ways. Some native people walked away with the English settlers' knives and cups. They didn't know that this was stealing. The settlers took over a nearby island that belonged to the native people. The settlers didn't know the island was special to them.

When winter came, the settlers didn't
have enough food. Native warriors hid
outside the walls of Jamestown. They
were waiting to shoot arrows at anyone
who left the fort. Within months, half
of the English were dead from hunger,
fever, or wounds.

One of the settlers was brave enough to go looking for food. He was Captain John Smith, an explorer who had traveled to many strange lands.

Smith and two other settlers found an Indian guide with a canoe. They were ready to travel deep into Powhatan's kingdom. They wanted to find a tribe with corn to trade.

They didn't get far. A party led by one of Pocahontas's brothers came upon the strangers. Two of the Englishmen were killed on the spot.

The native people could tell by
Smith's clothes and bold manners that
he was an important person, a chief.
They decided to take him prisoner.

John Smith was kept prisoner in Weromocomoco. After a few days, he was brought to Powhatan in his longhouse. The great chief sat on a low platform. He wore a cloak of raccoon skins. Around his neck were long strands of pearls. The men and women of his court sat around him.

In the center of the room were two large stones. Several Indians grabbed Captain Smith and stretched him out across the stones. Other Indians stood by, ready to beat him to death with clubs.

Suddenly, there was a shout. Pocahontas ran from the crowd. She threw herself on top of Smith.

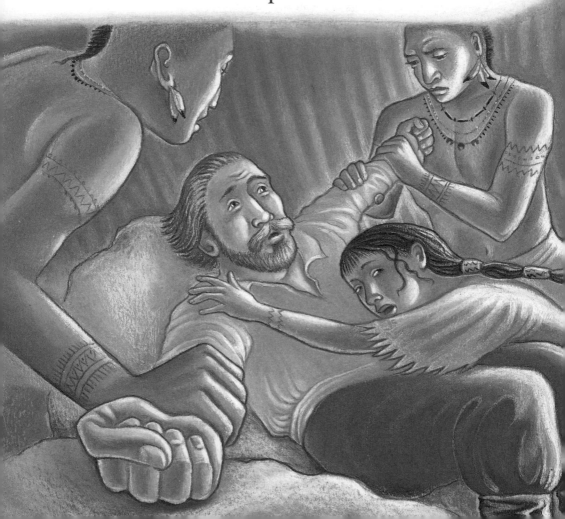

The Indians put down their clubs. They had to. Pocahontas had saved his life.

Women had the right to save a prisoner's life by adopting him. Pocahontas made John Smith an honorary relative.

Why did Pocahontas decide to rescue Captain Smith? Legend says that she had fallen in love with him. But maybe not. Pocahontas was just 11 or 12 years old. Her father probably had told her to do it. Killing a rival chief meant all-out war. And the English had guns. All that his warriors had were bows and arrows.

Powhatan let John Smith return to
Jamestown. Later, he sent Pocahontas to
the English fort. Her friends carried gifts
of corn and deer meat.

Pocahontas made many visits to
Jamestown. There were a few boys her
age at the fort. Pocahontas challenged
them to footraces. They taught her to
turn cartwheels.

Pocahontas taught Captain Smith to speak her language. He taught her many words of English.

The great chief's daughter was growing into a young woman. She no longer played childish games. She wore white feathers in her hair. They were the sign of a princess.

When Pocahontas looked at Captain Smith, her dark eyes lit up. Did she have a crush on the brave explorer? Maybe so. No one knows for sure. If she did, Captain Smith didn't seem to notice. He was too busy trying to keep the settlers alive.

One day a ship arrived. The captain had brought gifts for Powhatan from the king of England. There was a red wool suit, a brass crown, and a huge bed.

Smith was very unhappy about the choice of gifts. He knew that the crown was not a good gift. Powhatan would not like it. And getting that bed up the river was a lot of hard work.

When the Englishmen finally reached Powhatan's village, they heard wild screams coming from the woods. They were terrified.

But Pocahontas came to Captain Smith's side. She was laughing.

"Don't be afraid," she told him.

Then a group of girls came rushing out into the clearing. They wore antlers on their heads and dresses made of leaves. They did a wild dance of welcome. It was in honor of the visitors.

But the rest of the visit did not go well. Powhatan understood why the king was giving him a crown. The English king thought that this gift would make Powhatan loyal to him.

Powhatan refused to kneel so that the brass crown could be put on his head. The great Powhatan didn't kneel for anyone!

Powhatan saw now that the English were never going to leave his kingdom. He would have to make them leave.

The next time Smith visited Weromocomoco, he came to bargain for corn. While he was doing this, Powhatan and his family quietly left their longhouse and went deep into the forest.

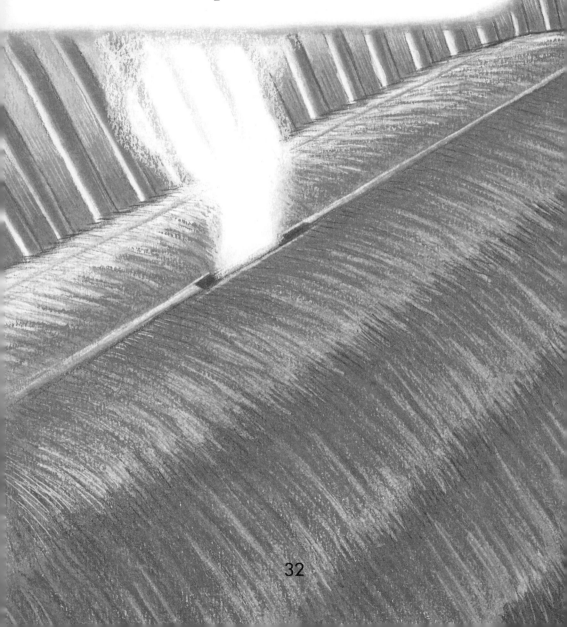

That night, Pocahontas crept back into the village where Smith and his men were camped. She was crying. Her father's warriors were preparing an ambush, she said. Powhatan had taken his family into the forest so they would be safe during the battle.

At midnight, Smith and his men
sneaked back to their boat and sailed
to Jamestown on the high tide.

Pocahontas had saved Smith's life
a second time!

But John Smith's days at Jamestown were coming to an end. Many settlers were angry with him for making them work so hard. They even accused him of wanting to marry Pocahontas to make himself king of Virginia.

About that time, Smith was burned in a fire. He was injured and he was tired. Soon, he sailed home to England.

Captain Smith had been tough but fair. Once he was gone, there was more trouble than ever.

That winter became known as the "starving time." Many of the settlers died.

Pocahontas heard a rumor that John Smith was dead. She was very sad.

Ships arrived from England in time to save Jamestown. Still, the settlers and the native people continued to fight.

Powhatan and his warriors took
some settlers prisoner. They captured
English guns, too.

Three years went by. One day, an English captain named Argall was on a trip up the coast when he heard that Pocahontas was nearby. Captain Argall got a friendly chief to get the princess to board the ship. Once she was on board, Pocahontas became Argall's prisoner.

Pocahontas was kept on a farm near Jamestown. The settlers sent a message to Powhatan. He must give back the English prisoners and the guns he had taken. Then he could have his daughter back.

The great chief said no.

When Pocahontas heard her father's answer, her heart was broken. She set aside her feathered robe and put on English clothes. She began to study the Bible and to learn English prayers. She even took a new name, Rebecca.

A year later, in 1614, she married an English settler named John Rolfe. They had a baby boy. He was named Thomas.

Once he had an English son-in-law, Powhatan became more friendly. He stopped making war on the English. The settlers talked about the "peace of Pocahontas."

John Rolfe decided to take his wife and baby home to England for a visit. Powhatan sent along a dozen Indians to travel with Pocahontas.

All of London went wild for Pocahontas and the Indians from Virginia. Princess Pocahontas was invited to the palace. She became a great friend of the English queen.

The king even sent a coach and horses to bring Pocahontas to a Christmas ball.

One day, an old friend paid Pocahontas a visit. It was Captain John Smith!

Why had he waited so long to come see her? Smith hadn't forgotten that people in Virginia accused him of wanting to marry Pocahontas. What would her husband think of that?

When Pocahontas saw John Smith, she turned her face away and left the room. Two hours passed before she was calm enough to talk. Then she cried out that her husband and his friends had lied to her. "They did tell us always you were dead!" She also told Smith, "I will be forever and ever your countryman."

The other people from her tribe couldn't wait to go home to Virginia. But not Pocahontas. She longed to stay in England, in the country of John Smith.

As the time to return home drew near, Pocahontas fell ill. She coughed all day and all night. Still, she had to go where her husband went. When spring came, she boarded the ship that would carry them back to the New World.

But before the ship reached the open sea, Pocahontas had died.

Pocahontas was buried in England. John Rolfe took their son Thomas back home to Virginia. To this day, there are families in Virginia who can trace their history back to this early American princess.

And now you know the true story of Pocahontas.